IRISH LIFE AND CULTURE

SAG

ANCIENT IRELAND

laoċra, Ríċe agus déiċe

Searóid ó Murċaḋa

do scríoḃ

Réamḟocal ag Nessa Ní Shé

Arna ċur amaċ do Ċomar Cultúra Éireann
ag Cló Mercier, 4 Sráid an Droiċid, Corcaiġ.

SAGA AND MYTH IN ANCIENT IRELAND

by

GERARD MURPHY

FOREWORD BY NESSA NÍ SHÉ

PUBLISHED FOR THE CULTURAL RELATIONS
COMMITTEE OF IRELAND BY THE MERCIER
PRESS, 4 BRIDGE STREET, CORK

S.B.N.   85342   268   0

First edition 1961
Reprinted 1971

The aim of this series is to give a broad, informed survey of Irish Life and culture, past and present. Each writer is left free to deal with his subject in his own way, and the views expressed are not necessarily those of the Committee. The general editor of the series is Caoimhín Ó Danachair.

The late Gerard Murphy wrote and lectured extensively on Irish literature of all periods. He was Professor of the History of Celtic Literature at University College, Dublin. From 1939 until his death in 1959 he was editor of Éigse, a scholarly journal of Irish studies published for the National University of Ireland by Colm O Lochlainn at the Sign of the Three Candles.

A bibliography of his publications is printed in Éigse, X (1961), 2-10.

Printed and bound in the Republic of Ireland by the Book Printing Division of Smurfit Print and Packaging Limited, Dublin

WHEN this book was first published in 1955 Professor
Murphy's list of works suggested for further reading
showed how little there had been published in the way of
early Irish literature. It is gratifying, therefore, to be able
to add to that list the result of an increasing interest in the
literature. With the publication of Professor James
Carney's *Studies in Irish Literature and History* (Dublin 1955)
an entirely new interpretation of the subject was offered.
Carney, rejecting nearly all the judgments of previous
scholars who held that the early Irish sagas have their roots
in ancient oral tradition, regards the sagas as being literature in the literal sense of the word composed by Irish
monks familar with the classical and Christian literature of
early Ireland; only to a small extent are they based on
oral tradition. Although several scholars, including Professor Murphy, were not in sympathy with the general
line of Carney's thought,[1] nevertheless, his criticism of
the generally accepted beliefs has stimulated further studies
of the Irish literary tradition.

A notable contribution to this field is Professor Proinsias
Mac Cana's comprehensive study (in *Celtica* vii [1966]
65–90) of the 'rhetoric'–those obscurely-worded phrases
in *Táin Bó Cúailnge* and other early Irish stories mentioned
by Professor Murphy, pp. 34, 48 infra. As these 'rhetorics'
are of special interest for their value as evidence for the
textual history of the *Táin*, Mac Cana's convincing argu-

1 For a review by Professor Murphy of Carney's book see
Éigse viii (1956), 152-64.

ment against a Latin origin for this *genre* in Irish literature—the notion held by Thurneysen and other scholars—is of considerable importance.[2]

The *Táin*, the central saga of the Ulster cycle and the nearest approach to a national epic, has engaged the attention of both Irish and European scholars since the beginning of the revival of interest in Irish literature. The climax to the work of all these scholars is Professor Cecile O'Rahilly's recent edition of *Táin Bó Cúalnge from the Book of Leinster* (Dublin 1966). In the opening pages of her Introduction Professor O'Rahilly investigates the question of oral tradition in the Heroic Saga in general with special reference to the *Táin*, and although she does not accept Professor Carney's main thesis she agrees with him on one point: heroic traditions preserved by scribes of a later age are inevitably influenced by the literary attainments of the compilers. Finally she states: 'If, however, we may postulate, as most scholars believe we can, a highly developed oral art of saga-recitation before the stories took literary form, then despite any influence on the saga-writers' technique or matter from written sources, we may conclude that the inspiration of the sagas is ultimately oral' (p.xiv).

2 In his study of this *genre* Professor Mac Cana shows that the early (and late) term for this form was *rosc(ad)* (originally denoting a 'vivid, memorable pronouncement'), the title *retoiric* (< Lat. *rhetorice*), not employed before the eleventh century, 'may be explained as a misreading of the abbreviation .r. (most likely by a redactor who was a little too conscious of his Latin learning)', *ibid.* p. 73.

But if scholars still hold differing views regarding the origin of the sagas there is more or less general agreement amongst them concerning the written traditions of stories, which, however, is at variance with the theory put forward by Professor Murphy in this book.

Professor Murphy regarded the manuscript versions of the tales as recorded lore, any artistry in the stories he attributed to the oral story-tellers, any defect to the monastic scribes. Thus he says ' . . . the stories are very imperfectly narrated in the manuscripts and not infrequently in a way that definitely suggests recording from an oral source,' (p. 12 infra), and a 'poorly-narrated manuscript version is often a mere 'summary of incidents rather than a tale meant to hold the interest of an audience by its artistry' (p. 15 infra). Comments of a similar nature will be found on pp. 13–14, 17, 28, 39, 49, 59, 62 infra.

Commenting on Murphy's opinions Professor Gearóid S. Mac Eoin says: 'The theory that these stories, in any form, were written down from dictation must be abandoned. It is altogether unnecessary, for there were in the monasteries, from the eighth century on, men well versed in historical traditions. These could have written the sagas in the form in which we have them without recourse to a narrator'[3] (*Studia Hibernica* vii [1967] 247). This observation has been re-affirmed by Professor Mac Cana in a

3 A similar suggestion in the case of the modern Irish Romantic Tales is made by Dr. Alan Bruford: 'With the exception of a few stories first written down about 1800 . . . there is no reason to suppose that any story as it stands in the manuscripts is a written-down folk-tale', *Béaloideas* xxxiv (1969).

recent essay on *Irish Literary Tradition* where he states that 'it is abundantly clear that they' [i.e. the Christian clerics] 'were far from being mere *amanuenses* in the service of oral tradition' (Ó Cuív, *A View of the Irish Language* [1969], p.42).

When Professor Murphy invokes 'the growing weariness of the reciter' (p. 12–13 infra) to explain the tailing off and poor ending of many stories Professor Mac Eoin, on the other hand, asks (ibid. 247) 'how many instances of this are there which cannot be ascribed to faulty textual transmission? And in how many instances is the ending really faulty and not merely different from what our twentieth-century canons would sanction?' Because 'it should be remembered that these stories, for the men who handed them down, were not detached pieces of fiction but part of the history of their people and that very often the end of a story consists of a tailpiece which connects the story with the general stream of traditions.' This apparently would explain the ending of *Scéla Mucce Maic Dá Thó* which Professor Murphy sees as 'a condensed summary of the succeeding events' (p.49 infra) but which Professor Mac Eoin would explain as the 'many loose ends, historical and onomastic' which the writer had to tie up, thereby continuing the story for a couple of paragraphs.
Although the endings of other stories are not capable of such a neat interpretation, nevertheless the faulty endings are not so common as to require Professor Murphy's theory to explain them.

No change has been made in the body of Professor Murphy's text but an attempt has been made to bring the references in the footnotes up to date. A list of books and essays suggested for further reading—other than those already mentioned in the Foreword, the text and the footnotes—is given at the end. A full bibliography up to 1942 will be found in the two volumes compiled by R. I. Best: National Library of Ireland, *Bibliography of Irish Philology and Literature* (1913), *Bibliography of Irish Philology and Manuscript Literature* (1942).

Nessa Ní Shé.

Abbrevations

RC   =*Revue Celtique*
ZCP   =*Zeitschrift für celtische Philologie*

SAGA AND MYTH IN
ANCIENT IRELAND

BY

GERARD MURPHY

STORYTELLING IN ANCIENT IRELAND

IRISH storytelling has always specially attracted the student of antiquity. In it he finds something unique in European tradition, a rich mass of tales depicting a West-European barbaric civilisation as yet uninfluenced by the mighty sister-civilisation of Graeco-Roman lands. Likewise, the lover of literature, having exhausted the possibilites of the maturer literatures of other countries, finds in Irish story-telling something to delight him from the youth of the world, before the heart had been trained to bow before the head or the imagination to be troubled by logic and reality: Cú Chulainn, abandoning his watch over the frontiers of Ulster to keep a pledged tryst with the King of Tara's wife, need fear no implied rebuke from the narrator of his deeds, and the strange impact on the human world of the spirit folk who dwell unseen by men in the hills beside them is accepted as part of an order which men as yet have neither sought to understand nor rebelled against by reason of its injustice.

Though our knowledge of ancient Irish storytelling comes mainly from manuscript versions of the tales, there can be little doubt that Irish narrative tradition has on the whole been essentially oral. That this was the universal rule ar least till the middle of the seventh century no scholar would deny. That it has also been the rule for two hundred years past, both in Ireland and Gaelic Scotland, where the folktale is concerned, is also an undeniable fact. Thurneysen, however, author of what will for long remain the standard treatise on ancient Irish storytelling,[1] believed that from the eighth and ninth centuries on the main body of Irish narrative tradition was propagated normally by means of manuscripts.

Now Thurneysen in the work referred to, has undoubtedly proved that the manuscript tradition of a tale, once it had received written form seems normally to have been carried on, in the manuscripts, independently of oral tradition, though this is not the case so universally as he would have held. As has been pointed out, however, in *Ériu*, XVI (1952), 152, the tendency of scribes to reproduce an already written text no more disproves the existence of a living oral tradition than the tendency of folklorists of the last generation to use Curtin as their source disproves the fact that a vigorous oral tradition of folktale-telling is still being carried on in Gaelic-speaking districts wholly un-

1 R. Thurneysen, *Die irische Helden - und Königsage*, I-II (1921). For Thurneysen's view of the relationship of manuscript and oral tradition see especially pp. 72-73. For arguments against it see *Ériu*, XVI (1952), 151-2. A more general presentation of the case for oral transmission of Irish tales will be found in *Duanaire Finn*, III (ed. G. Murphy), 189-192.
For a more recent study of this subject see A. Bruford, *Béaloideas* XXXIV (1969).

influenced by Curtin's or any other folklorist's recordings.

Perhaps a stronger argument for the literary nature of Irish story-tradition, from the eighth and ninth centuries on, is the usage of the greater part of medieval Europe. But that Irish narrative tradition was different from that of medieval Europe rather than governed by the same laws, is strongly suggested by the written texts themselves, first because in those texts 'telling' and 'hearing' stories is commonly referred to, and secondly because as a rule the stories are very imperfectly narrated in the manuscripts and not infrequently in a way that definitely suggests recording from an oral source.[2]

The artistry of the modern Gaelic storyteller is often remarkable, and the critical spirit of his peasant audience highly developed. Professor James H. Delargy is therefore right when he suggests that the more cultivated audiences of the Irish middle ages would not 'have listened very long to the storyteller if he were to recite tales in the form in which they have come down to us.'[3] Moreover several of the best manuscript texts begin well, but tail off badly as the story proceeds. This strange procedure can be easily explained on the hypothesis of recording from oral recitation.[4] Everyone who has tried to record Irish folktales from peasant reciters before the introduction of recording machines has noticed the curtailment and imperfection which tend gradually to creep into the recorded

2 This theory—that the manuscript versions of the tales is recorded lore—has recently been challenged. See Foreword p. 7.

3 *The Gaelic Story-teller* (1945), 32.

4 See note 2 supra.

narrative owing to the growing weariness of the reciter. Recorders in other countries have been acutely aware of the same phenomenon. Radlov, a collecter of Tartar epic poetry, has for instance, been quoted as follows by H. M. and Mrs. Chadwick in their *Growth of Literature, III* (1940), 180:

> In spite of all my efforts I have not succeeded in reproducing the poetry of the minstrels completely. The repeated singing of one and the same song, the slow dictation, and my frequent interuptions often dispersed the excitement which is necessary to the minstrel for good singing. He was only able to dictate in a tired and negligent way what he had produced for me a little before with fire.

And the Chadwicks themselves a few pages later (183) say that 'the weariness of the singer, and the consequent lapses of memory and flagging narrative are constantly brought home to us as we draw towards the close of Radlov's poems, which offer a striking contrast to their brilliant opening scenes.'

When we think of the well-constructed narratives which even the unlearned peasant narrator to-day can produce, and when we judge of the greater power of Old Irish story-tellers by consideration of certain passages scattered through the inartistic manuscript versions of their tales which have been preserved, we can be fairly certain that the tales, as really told to assembled kings and noblemen at an ancient *óenach*, were very different from the poorly-narrated manuscript versions noted down by monastic scribes as a

13

contribution to learning rather than to literature.[5]

The ninth-century story of Cano son of Gartnán[6] offers a good example. Its opening paragraph leads the reader to expect exquisite artistry in the tale as a whole:

> Áedan son of Gabrán, and Gartnán son of Áed, were contending for the kingship of Scotland, and half the men of Scotland fell between them in fights and battles. Gartnán lived in Inis Macu Chéin.[7] That island was covered with the best buildings in the western part of the world. Every house on the island all around it, including the privy, was of strip-work laid over beams of red yew from peak to peak in Gartnán's time. Gartnán had his whole island gilded with red gold. On the arable land he had seven plough-teams. He had seven herds with seven score cows in each herd. He had fifty nets for deer, and out from the island were fifty nets for fishing. The fifty fish-nets had ropes from them over the windows of the kitchen. There was a bell at the end of each rope, on the rail, in front of the steward. Four men used to throw (?) the first-run salmon up to him. He himself in the meantime drank mead upon his couch.

5 For critcism of this opinion see Foreword p. 7.

6 Ed. D. A. Binchy, *Scéla Cano Meic Gartnáin* (1963). An English translation is given by K. Meyer, *Anecdota from Irish Manuscripts* I (1907), 1-15, a summary of the tale by M. Dillon, *The Cycle of the Kings* (1946). It is modernised by P. Mac Cana, *Scéalaoícht na Ríthe* (1956).

7 To-day Skye.

About page 2 of the printed text one begins to suspect that elaborate descriptions of this sort are being hinted at rather than recorded, and from page 3 on, the story begins to resemble a summary of incidents rather than a tale meant to hold the interest of an audience by its artistry.[8]

The printed text would take about half an hour to recite. Modern folktales as told by good storytellers often take an hour to recite, and some of them may even be spun out to last for several sessions.[9] Moreover it is the long tale which is most highly thought of to-day by Gaelic peasant audiences,[10] and similar love of length has been commented on by collectors of oral literature in other regions.[11] We should hardly be far wrong, therefore, in conjecturing that the Story of Cano son of Gartnán as really told in the ninth century would have contained many elaborate passages reminiscent of the opening passage just quoted, would have been much better knit than the manuscript version, and would have taken an hour or several hours to tell. Moreover, in the tale as originally told, not the opening, but some episode in the middle or end would probably have most awakened our admiration. For it is the law of oral narration that the story improves as the appreciation of the audience begins to affect the narrator.[12]

8 For criticism of this opinion see Foreword p. 7.
9 J. H. Delargy, *The Gaelic Story-teller*, 21-22.
10 *Ib.*, 34.
11 Cf. the Chadwicks, *l.c.*, 185.
12 'The sympathy of the hearers always spurs the minstrel to new efforts of strength,' writes Radlov of Tartar epic poetry (Chadwicks, *l.c.*, 184).

Whereas modern French story-tradition, let us say, is purely literary, and thirteenth-century French story-tradition, in so far as the reciter had derived his text from a manuscript, is essentially literary, it is unlikely that Irish srory-tradition before the seventeenth century depended to any large extent upon manuscripts.[13] Medieval Irish manuscripts would seem indeed to be related to living story-telling much as the museum to-day is related to living material culture. The manuscripts contain samples from interesting specimens of genuine storytelling, particularly from out-of-date specimens, arranged without much attention to artistic requirememts, just as the museum contains samples of out-of-date furniture and household utensils arranged with a view to antiquarian instruction rather than to suit the purposes of real life.

In 1940 Domhnall Bán Ó Céileachair, a West Cork farmer, published an autobiography[14] which he had dictated to his sons and daughters, who were then school-children. In the process of correcting the script in preparation for having it printed, Domhnall Bán's wife was often present and would sometimes complain that such an episode had not been suitably narrated. Domhnall Bán would usually admit the defect and begin to narrate the episode orally. Had he been able, at the moment of dictating, to capture the fire and eloquence of the moment of oral narration, and had the scribes been able to record what he said, how much more excellent would that excellent

13 For criticism of this opinion see A. Bruford, *op. cit.*, 4 et passim.

14 Domhnall Bán Ó Céileachair, *Sgéal mo Bheatha,*

autobiography have been! But such a combination was, alas, impossible. If it was impossible in the days of steel pen, paper jotter, printing press and paper book, how much more impossible was it in the days of the *stilus*, waxed tablet, quill pen, and vellum codex! When therefore we form a picture of the orally narrated Irish tale as something immeasurably superior to the suggestions of it a monastic scribe has recorded,[15] we are not creating a figment of the imagination, we are merely restoring to the corpse buried in a manuscript the soul that once animated it.

Sgéalaighe (as the word for storyteller is spelt in Modern Irish) to-day awakens thoughts of an unlettered fisherman or farmer telling folktales by a cottage fireside. To the ninth-century authors of the Exile of the Sons of Uisliu,[16] however, or to the late-twelfth-century author of the poem on Gréssach, the Túatha Dé Danann storyteller, contained in the fourteenth-century Book of Uí Maine,[17] the word *scélaige* would have more aristocratic associations. Feidlimid mac Daill, Conchobar's pre-Christian *scélaige* in the Exile of the Sons of Uisliu, is represented, for instance, as entertaining princes in his house and as having a daughter, Deirdre, who was a fitting consort for a king. Indeed, from the differences observable between different genres of storytelling, from references in literary texts to storytellers of different ranks in society, and from analogy with the first steps of an ascending scale still to be noticed in Gaelic-

15 For criticism of this opinion see Foreword p. 7.

16 Ed. V. Hull, *Longes Mac n-Uislenn* (1949) with English translation, 43 and 60, §1.

17 Facsimile, 157a8 (=216a8).

2

speaking districts,[18] it may be concluded that in ancient Ireland a whole hierarchy of storytellers existed, ranging from the humble teller of folktales to the *fili*, who as well as being a learned poet, master of *senchus* (history) and *dinnshenchus* (placelore), had been trained to narrate 'the chief stories of Ireland to kings, lords, and noblemen.'[19] From a text in eighth-century Irish, for example[20], we learn that Mongán son of Fiachna, an East Ulster king who died about A.D.625, was told a story by his *fili*, Forgoll, every winter night from *Samuin* to *Beltaine* (1st November to 1st May).

Irish scribes of all periods have tended to record in their manuscripts only the lore of whatever happened to be the most learned class of their day. We may take it, therefore, that the type of storytelling which we see imperfectly reflected in medieval manuscripts is on the whole that of the *fili*, who in real life told his tales at their best in the *oénaige* (fairs), where, under the patronage of kings and the sanction of age-old custom, the arts of early Ireland seem to have received their fullest expression.[21]

18 *Duanaire Finn*, III (ed. G. Murphy), xxxvii-xxxix, 189-192.

19 *Is hí dano foglaim na hochtmaide bliadna . . . ocus dín[n]shenchus ocus primscéla Hérend olchena fria naisnéis do ríghaib ocus flaithib ocus dagdhoínib* (The matter learnt in the eighth year [of a poet's training] consisted of . . . and placelore and the chief stories of Ireland also, to narrate them to kings and lords and noblemen), *Mittelirische Verslebren*, II, §91, ed. Thurneysen in Stokes and Windisch's *Irsche Texte*, III (1891), 50.

20 K. Meyer, *Voyage of Bran*, (1895), 45-46. Cf. Thurneysen, *Heldensage* (1912), 67.

21 *Studies*, March 1940, 22-23.

Twelfth-century *filid* divided the tales they told into *prímscéla* and *fo-scéla*, main tales and subsidiary tales; and, though the numbers are hardly to be taken as exact, they claimed to know in all seven times fifty (350) tales, of which five fifties (250) were main tales, and two fifties (100) subsidiary tales. Comparatively few of the tales have been preserved to the present day, but two long lists of the titles of main tales, representing perhaps the repertory of tenth-century *filid*, with some eleventh and twelfth-century additions, are extant to-day, as well as a third similar summary list. [22] In the lists, the tales are classified by the first words of their titles into *Togla* (destructions), *Tána* (cattle-raids), *Tochmarca* (wooings), *Catha* (battles), *Uatha* (caves),[23] *Immrama* (voyages), *Aitte* (deaths), *Fessa* (feasts), *Forbasa* (sieges), *Echtrai* (adventure-journeys), *Aitheda* (elopements), *Airgne* (slaughters), *Tomadmann* (eruptions), *Slúagaid* (expeditions), *Tochomlada* (immigrations), *Físi* (visions), and *Serca* (love-tales). Modern scholars, however, prefer to classify the stories partly according to their subject-matter and partly according to their spirit into Mythological tales, Heroic tales, King tales, Finn tales, and Romantic tales.

In this booklet an attempt will be made to describe the Mythological tales, the Heroic tales, and the King tales.

22 Thurneysen, *op. cit.*, 21-24.

23 Cf. Early Modern *fuathacha* 'holes (in the ground)', *Regimen na Sláinte* (*Regimen Sanitatis Magnini Mediolanensis*), ed. S. Ó Ceithearnaigh, II, 5665, 5834. The *Uatha*, most of which are wholly lost, seem to refer to incidents which took place in famous caves.

Finn tales and Romantic tales received their greatest development after the Old and Middle Irish periods.[24] They will therefore be treated of in a separate booklet, to be entitled The Ossianic Lore and Romantic Tales of Medieval Ireland.

MYTHOLOGICAL TALES

From the oldest period of Irish tradition down to the present day Irish storytellers speak currently of a spirit folk living close to human beings, but normally concealed from them. They are the *des síde* of Old Irish tradition, known in spoken Irish as the *slúagh sídhe* (*síodh*-host), *slúagh aérach* (airy host), *bunadh na gcnoc* (hill folk), *daoine maithe* (good people), etc., and in English as the fairies. From ancient times they have been looked upon as dwelling either in certain hills called *sídi* (Modern Irish *sídhe* or *síodha*, from which conception comes their name *des síde*, 'people of the *sídi*'), or in far-away islands, or beneath the waters of the sea or of lakes. To the learned in Gaelic Ireland the *des síde*, were known as *Túatha Dé Donann* (later *Danann*), which originally meant the Peoples of the Goddess Donu.[25]

When in poetic and storytelling mood even the learned made little or no attempt to conceal the fact that the Túatha Dé Donann were a spirit folk. When in historical mood, however, they euhemerized them into a human race,

24 Old Irish, c.600-c.900; Middle Irish, c.900-c.1200; Early Modern Irish, c.1200-c.1650.

25 See *Duanaire Finn*, III, 208-210.

skilled in magic, who once occupied Ireland but were defeated by the invading *Goídil* or Gaels. Stories which introduce the *áes síde* or Túatha Dé Donann as principle actors are to-day known as Mythological tales, for to the modern scholar it is clear that the Túatha Dé Donann and *áes síde* were the gods of pagan Ireland surrounded by the lesser divinities and spirits over whom they ruled. Many of the chief persons among them are identifiable with Celtic gods known to us from other sources: *Lug*, for instance, with the god who gave his name to Lyons (Lugdunum,) Laon, Leyden, and other continental towns;[26] and *Núadu* with the *Nodons* (or *Nodens*) who was worshipped in a Romano-British temple at Lydney Park in Gloucestershire.[27] The divine nature of others among them is guaranteed by ancient Irish tradition: thus Cormac, king and bishop of Cashel about the year 900, states in his Glossary that Manannán was god of the sea (*inde Scotti et Brittones eum deum vocaverunt maris*); and the same writer suggests the Dagda's divinity by saying that the Dagda's daughter Brigit, patroness of poetry, was adored as a goddess.[28] Indeed the Dagda's name, which originally would have meant 'good god', in itself suggests his godhood, while the fact that his daughter Brigit, patroness of poetry, had two sisters, also called Brigit and patronesses respectively

26 *l.c.*, lxxiv-lxxvi.

27 A. C. L. Brown, *The Origin of the Grail Legend* (1943), 146; R. A. S. Macalister, *Lebor Gabála Érenn*, IV (1941), 97-98.

28 There can be little doubt but that she is the same as the *dea Brigantia* of Roman Britain: cf. Dottin, *Religion des Celts* (1908), 20, and Vendryes, *La Religion des Celtes* (1948), 272.

21

of law and smithcraft, reminds one of the tendency of the Gallic Celts to present their divinities in triadic form.[29] Moreover the background and atmosphere of the tales, redolent of marvel, preternatural power and strange loveliness, are such as one would expect in a mythological cycle. In this respect the Irish mythological tales remind one of the Welsh *Mabinogion*, in which many Túatha Dé Donann names occur in Welsh form,—*Donu* as *Don*,[30] *Mac ind Óc* as *Mabon*,[31] *Lug* as *Lleu*, *Núadu* as *Nudd*, *Manannán* as *Manawydan*, *Giobniu* as *Govannon*,—suggesting that the spirit and some of the characters of the two groups of tales go back to the primitive paganism once shared by these two Celtic peoples.

In tales of the Irish Mythological cycle we may therefore expect to find much of the mythology of the primitive Celts. It is to be noted, however, that mythology, largely the creation of poets and storytellers, gives little information concerning the essential elements of a people's religion. From what Homer tells us of the loves and enmities of the Olympians ruled over by Zeus we could, for instance, learn but little of religious rites such as the Eleusinian mysteries and of the various feasts and sacrifices by which the Athenian citizen in the fifth century B.C. hoped to ensure the well-being of himself and his city. Greek myths as preserved for us by Roman poets are still further divorced from religion understood in the true sense of the

29 Dottin, *l.c.*, 25.

30 *Duanaire Finn*, III, lxxxiii, 208-210, 447.

31 T. F. O'Rahilly, *The Goidels and their Predecessors* (1935), 38.

22

word. Many Irish mythological tales have survived through the Christian ages by reason of their value as stories; but, as remembered by the Christian Irish, they throw no more light on ancient Celtic religion than the Roman versions of Greek myths, unaided by Greek religious monuments, would throw on ancient Greek religion. Neglect of this consideration has led to several unjustified conclusions concerning primitive Irish religion. E. J. Gwynn,[32] for instance, believed that the absence of 'evidence of ritual, or worship or prayer or sacrifice,' indicated a religion among the Gaels 'unworthy of their general level of culture,' and A. G. van Hamel[33] that, where other peoples gave religious cult to gods, the Celts used to tell what he calls Exemplary Myths concerning protection of the land in past time by Heroes, these Exemplary Myths being intended partly to teach kings how to carry out their task of actually protecting the land in the present, partly to bring about, by the mere recitation of them, recurrence of the victories and blessings which were the Heroes' lot. Avoiding similar rash conclusions, we shall in this booklet discuss the Mythological tales for their story value only, making little or no attempt to relate them to the fundamental religious beliefs and practices of the pagan Celts.

Of all the Mythological tales that entitled *Cath Maige*

32 See pp. 54 and 55 of *The Church of Ireland, A.D. 432-1932* (Report of the Church of Ireland Conference . . . 1932).

33 In his *Aspects of Celtic Mythology* (1934). For criticism of van Hamel's opinions see *Duanaire Finn* III, 213-217.

Tuired, the Battle of Moytirra,[34] is of greatest interest to students of Irish mythology, for in it almost the whole Irish pantheon appears. Its theme, a battle in which the Túatha Dé Donann defeat the Fomoiri, is reminiscent of Greek traditions concerning the defeat inflicted on Cronus and his Titans by Zeus and the Olympian gods, or of

34 Moytirra (East and West) are two townlands near Lough Arrow, Co. Sligo. The tale discussed in the present booklet was originally referrd to simply as *Cath Maige Tuired*. Later it is sometimes called *Cath Dédenach Maige Tuired* (The Last Battle of M. T.) or *Cath Tánaiste Maige Tuired* (The Second Battle of M. T.), and later still *Cath Maighe Tuireadh Thúaidh* (The Battle of Northern M. T.). These names are used to distinguish it from another battle, in which, according to eleventh-century historical doctrine, the Túatha Dé Donann won Ireland from the Fir Bolg, twenty-seven years before defeating the Fomoiri in the more famous battle here under consideration. The battle against the Fir Bolg is often called *Cét-chath Maige Tuired* (The First Battle of M. T.). To distinguish it still more clearly from the more famous battle with the Fomoiri it was ultimately decided that it was fought at a different 'plain of pillars' near Cong, Co. Mayo, about fifty miles south-west of the original Moytirra: this explains the late names *Cath Maighe Tuireadh Cunga* (The Battle of M. T. of Cong), and *Cath Maighe TuireadhTheas* (The Battle of Southern M.T.).

For the location of *Mag Tuired* ('Plain of Pillars', now called Moytirra), and for references to the names given the two battles, see T. F. O'Rahilly, *Early Ir. Hist. and Mythol.* (1964), 388-390. For arguments against T. F. O'Rahilly's thesis that 'the story of the first battle of Mag Tuired was in existence before that of the second, to which it served as model', see *Éigse*, VII (1954), 191 sq.

Scandinavian traditions concerning wars between Aesir and Vanir.

The Fomoiri are normally pictured as unpleasant spirits dwelling overseas to the north of Ireland. There is a vagueness, however, in Irish tradition concerning them which is in marked contrast with the clear characterisation and wealth of detail about individuals which has been handed down concerning the Túatha Dé Donann. Indeed the vagueness is such that it has permitted so great an expert as T. F. O'Rahilly to suggest that between the Fomoiri and the Túatha Dé 'there is at bottom no real distinction.'[35] Greek tradition concerning the Titans, however, when compared with Greek tradition concerning the Olympian gods, is marked by a similar vagueness. Moreover the Fomoiri, like the Titans, are in Irish tradition consistently pictured in an unfavourable light, and when they are specifically referred to as Fomoiri they are as consistently opposed to the Túatha Dé as the Greek Titans are to the Olympian gods. It would seem therefore that a similar contrast between two groups of spirits, and traditions of a battle between them, go back to the days of primitive Indo-European unity and are not of such late origin as O'Rahilly would have had us believe.

Cath Maige Tuired is named in the three tale-lists mentioned *supra* (p. 19) as a tale that a *fili* should be able to tell. An idea of how it was told at different periods may be gained from reading the three extant manuscript tales connected with it.

35 O'Rahilly, *l.c.*, 524.

The oldest of these is entitled *Cath Maige Turedh ocus Genemain Bres Meic Elathain ocus a Rīghe*, 'The Battle of Moytirra, and the Birth of Bres Son of Elathan and His Reign'. It is preserved in the sixteenth-century British Museum manuscript, Harley 5280, f.63 sq., and has been edited with a translation by Stokes, RC, XII, 56 sq. Omissions in Stokes's edition have been supplied by Thurneysen, ZCP, XII, 401 sq. It would seem to be a composite work put together by an eleventh or twelfth-century redactor mainly from ninth-century material.

The second is entitled *Do Chath Mhuighe Tuireadh*,'Concerning the Battle of Moytirra.' It is preserved in the seventeenth-century Royal Irish Academy manuscript, 24 P 9, f.65 sq., and has been edited in booklet form by Brian Ó Cuív (1945). It deals with the immediate preparations for the battle and the battle itself, omitting the description of Bres's tyranny over the Túatha Dé and the coming of their saviour, Lug, described in the introductory portion of the older text. But the first paragraph of this second text clearly implies knowledge on the part of the reader of something corresponding to that introduction. This second manuscript tale was first written down probably in the thirteenth century. While in general theme it agrees with the older text, in style and in detail it is quite independent of it.

The third manuscript tale is entitled *Oidheadh Chloinne Tuireann*, 'The Death of the Children of Tuireann,' and is preserved in many eighteenth and nineteenth-century manuscripts. It describes the coming of Lug in a form completely different from that given in the old text and, in addition, as its main theme, the obtaining by the three sons of Tuireann, at Lug's behest, of magic articles to be used by him in the battle. It ends with an account of the death of the three sons of Tuireann, before the battle, as the result of wounds received by them in fulfilling their task. *Oidheadh Chloinne Tuireann* was certainly in existence in the sixteenth century,[36] and the main elements of it are all mentioned in some form or other between the eleventh and late fourteenth centuries.[37] As known to us from eighteenth and nineteenth-century manuscripts it would seem to represent late scribes' recensions of a text that was probably written down in a substantially similar form in the fourteenth century.[38]

The existence of these three manuscript tales, differing greatly from one another even when they describe the same incidents, and the existence of many different accounts of various incidents connected with the battle spread widely through the literature of all periods,[39] suggest both that *Cath Maige Tuired* was always a popular story and that the tradition of it was essentially oral, unified where the main theme was concerned, but, like all oral tradition, constantly varying in the manner of presentation of that theme and in the particular incidents introduced into it.

The oldest of these three manuscript tales is the longest and most interesting. Nevertheless it is probably the least

36 *Éigse*, IV, 249.

37 Flower, *Catalogue*, II, 348-349; O'Rahilly, *Early Ir. Hist. and Mythol.*, 308-317.

38 Cf. O'Rahilly, *l.c.*, 312, n.2.

39 See *Éigse*, VII, 196, n.3.

like any of the living methods of telling the story current at any period; for its juxtaposition of Old Irish and Middle Irish matter and its tendency to record stray scraps of lore about the characters mentioned, rather than to concentrate on episodes essential to the theme,[40] remind one forcibly of the museum type of arrangement, already referred to on p. 16, which is so common in manuscript texts of our older saga-tradition. Some passages, however, particularly that which narrates the coming of Lug (the Samildánach) from *Emain Ablach* ('Emain of the Apple-trees'—the Arthurian Avalon), when the Túatha Dé were most in need of him, may be used to form an idea of the artistry which doubt-less would have characterised the whole story as told at a ninth-century *óenach*:[41]

> The doorkeeper saw an unknown troop approaching him. A fair and shapely warrior, with a king's trappings was in the forefront of that band. They bade the doorkeeper to announce in Tara that they had come. 'Who is here?' said the doorkeeper. 'Here is Lug of the fierce combats, son of Cían son of Dían Cécht, and of Ethniu daughter of Balar; he is the fosterson of Talann, daughter of Magmór king of Spain, and of Echaid the Rough son of Duí.'

40 For comment on this see Foreword p. 7.

41 Commenting on this G. Mac Eoin says: 'There is no evidence that complete tales, as they would have been told at an *oenach* in, say the ninth century, were ever written down and I do not think that it has ever been claimed that any of the surviving sagas represents such a telling', *Studia Hibernica* VII, 247.

28

The doorkeeper asked the Samildánach:[42] 'What art dost thou practice? For no one without an art enters Tara.' 'Question me,' he said: 'I am a wright.' The doorkeeper answered: 'We need no wright. We have a wright already, Luchta son of Lúachaid.' He said: 'Question me, doorkeeper: I am a smith.' The doorkeeper answered him: 'We have a smith already, Colum Cúailleinech of the three new processes.' He said: 'Question me: I am a champion.' The doorkeeper answered: 'We need thee not. We have a champion already, Ogma son of Ethliu.' He said again: 'Question me: I am a harper.' 'We need thee not. We have a harper already, Abcán son of Bicelmos whom the Men of the Three Gods entertained in síd-mounds.' He said: 'Question me: I am a warrior.' The doorkeeper answered: 'We need thee not. We have a warrior already, Bresal Echarlam son of Echu Báeth-lám.' Then he said: 'Question me, doorkeeper: I am a poet and historian.' 'We need thee not: we have a poet and historian already, Én son of Ethoman.' He said: 'Question me: I am a sorcerer.' 'We need thee not. We have sorcerers already; our wizards and men of power are many.' He said: 'Question me: I am a leech.' 'We need thee not. As leech we already have Dían Cécht.' 'Question me,' said he: 'I am a cupbearer.' 'We need thee not. We already have

42 Ildánach means 'possessing many crafts.' The prefix sam, which occurs also before other adjectives, is taken by Stokes (RC, XII, 123) to mean 'together, at the same time.'

cupbearers, Delt and Drúcht and Daithe, Taí and Talam and Trog, Glé and Glan and Glése.' He said: 'Question me: I am a good metal-worker.' 'We need thee not: we already have a metal-worker, Credne the Metal-worker.' He spoke again saying: 'Ask the king whether he has one single man who possesses all these arts, and if he has I shall not enter Tara.'

The doorkeeper went into the palace and declared all to the king. 'A warrior has come before the garth,' said he, 'called Samildánach; and that one man possesses all the arts practiced by thy household so that he is the man of each and every art.' 'Let him into the garth,' said Núadu; 'for his like has never before come to this fortress.'

Then the doorkeeper let Lug pass him, and he went into the fortress and sat in the sage's seat, for he was a sage in every art.[43]

43 RC, XII, 74-78 (§53-71). A still more artistic telling of this episode is to be found in a poem begining *Mór ar bhfearg riot, a rí Saxan* ('Great is our wrath against thee, King of England'), written to honour Maurice FitzMaurice, second earl of Desmond, in the middle of the fourteenth century. The author of the poem, Gofraidh Fionn Ó Dálaigh, doubtless following the oral tradition of his day, makes Lug concentrate on his magic or acrobatic arts, such as 'leaping on a bubble without breaking it.' Though the doorkeeper in Gofraidh's poem is ordered by the Túatha Dé to admit Lug, Lug, to avoid breaking the *geis* or 'taboo' which forbade the fortress of Tara to be opened before sunrise, leaped over the rampart.

30

A sentence describing Lug's winning a game of *fidchell*,[44] which seems out of place in the context, and another sentence on the origin of that game, which is certainly due to a late glossator, have been omitted in the above citation. It is unlikely that anything corresponding to either sentence would have been heard in the story as told in the ninth century. It will be noticed too that the doorkeeper knows that Lug is called the Samildánach, though that name had not been given him in the conversation upon which his knowledge of the stranger's identity is supposed to be based. Such a lapse from the canons of good story-telling would hardly have occurred in a genuine telling of the tale.

Cath Maige Tuired gives us more information about individual members of the ancient Irish pantheon than any other single tale of the mythological cycle. The other-world atmosphere which gives its special beauty to that cycle is however, better illustrated in other tales, such as the ninth-century *Tochmarc Étaíne* or 'Wooing of Étaín,' which tells how Étaín, wooed and won by Midir in the otherworld, was transformed into a brilliantly-coloured fly by her rival Fúamnach, who blew her into this world, where, swallowed in a drink by an Ulster queen, she was reborn as a human. Wooed once more in human shape by the king of Tara, she was ultimately won back to the otherworld by Midir as the result of a rash stake made by the king in a game of *fidchell*.

44 The later Irish, including the author of this gloss, identified *fidchell*, a native board-game, with chess (See *Éigse*, V, 25).

Many tales, often with the word *Echtra*, 'adventure-journey', in their title, tell of the journeys of human beings to the otherworld. They tend to have a peculiar beauty by reason of the descriptions contained in them of the land 'where there is nought but truth, where there is neither age, nor decay, nor gloom, nor sadness, nor envy, nor jealousy, nor hate, nor pride.'[45] Though essentially mythological, they may be loosely connected with any cycle by reason of their human hero. Thus *Seirglige Con Culainn ocus Óenét Emire*, 'Cú Chulainn's Wasting Sickness and Emer's Only Jealousy', extant in a composite version which includes ninth-century and eleventh-century strata,[46] might by reason of the presence in it of Cú Chulainn, be classified with the Heroic tales. It tells of the love-sickness induced in Cú Chulainn by Fann, wife of Manannán, and Cú Chulainn's resultant journey to her court. This fairy mistress type of tale is still popular in Irish folklore.

Closely allied to the *Echtrai* are the *Immrama* or 'Voyages'. In them the otherworld is pictured as situated on islands in the western ocean. The earliest of them, the eighth-century *Immram Brain* or 'Voyage of Bran',[47] is essentially pagan in character. But by the ninth century the *Immrama* had been adapted to suit a Christian outlook and may

45 *Echtra Chormaic i dTír Tairngire* 'Cormac's Journey to the Land of Promise' (Stokes, *Irische Texte* III, 1891, 193, 212, late twelfth century). Modernised by T. Ó Floinn, *Scéalaíocht na Ríthe* (1956).

46 Ed. M. Dillon, *Serglige Con Culainn* (1953) with an English translation in *Scottish Gaelic Studies* VII (1951), 47-75.

47 Modernised by P. Mac Cana, *op. cit.*

describe the magic islands visited by Christian monks or penitents. On one of these Christianised *Immrama*, the ninth-century *Immram Maíle Dúin* or 'Voyage of Máel Dúin', a late-ninth or early-tenth-century Irish Latinist modelled his *Navigatio Brendani*, which, translated into many continental languages, became one of the most popular stories of the Middle Ages and played an important past in inspiring those real voyages which culminated in the discovery of America.

TALES OF THE HEROIC AGE

The Irish Mythological tales, and the Finn tales, which are closely related to them, are of special interest to students of the Welsh Mabinogion and the continental Arthurian tales; for owing to the conservatism of Irish tradition, the Celtic mythological themes and motifs which are common to them all are often preserved in a more primitive form in the Irish tales. Tales of the Heroic cycle are of interest for a different reason. They preserve a spirit and tradition which but for them would have been lost to Europe. For, while a spirit akin to that of the Irish Mythological cycle has become part of the general tradition of European literature through the medium of the French Arthurian cycle, the Irish Heroic cycle is unique in being the only branch of European literature which has preserved something of the warrior spirit and tradition of the ancient Celts as known to writers of classical antiquity. It is in Greek epic literature rather than in medieval romantic literature that the Irish Heroic tales find their closest parallels.

33

H. M. Chadwick in his *Heroic Age*, and later in various chapters of *The Growth of Literature*, written by him in collaboration with his wife, Mrs. N. K. Chadwick, has pointed out that a type of literature commonly described as Heroic is to be found in many languages. While in style it may vary from the poetic perfection of the Greek *Iliad* to the prose ornamented with speech-poetry and 'rhetorics'[48] in which the Irish *Táin Bó Cúailnge* is presented, in matter and in the structure of its narrative it is almost everywhere the same. Heroic literature is aristocratic in outlook. As virtues it recognises loyalty, prowess, and fulfilment of one's word. Boasting, provided that the boast be equalled by the deed, is not considered a fault. It idealises its heroes, yet remains fundamentally realistic: those heroes are made of flesh and blood; their success or failure depends more on character and action than on accident or magic, though fate and the gods may be regarded as inscrutable yet necessary factors in life. War is the profession of the princes of whom it treats, a type of war which is direct and straightforward, almost devoid of strategy, and commonly decided by the personal prowess of leaders. Description of the ceremony of court life, of the interior of palaces, and of the ornament of clothes and weapons, is universal in heroic literature.

Chadwick has identified some of the central figures of Teutonic heroic literature with barbarian leaders mentioned

48 Utterances of druids or heroes in obscurely worded alliterative prose often with archaic or artificial word-order.

For a comprehensive study of this *genre* in Irish literature see P. Mac Cana, *Celtica* VII, (1966), 65–90. See also Foreword pp. 5–6.

by historians of the later Roman Empire. In his *Heroic Age* he had shown that the heroic poetry of the Jugoslavs is about persons of whose historic existence there can be no doubt, and that at least the material civilisation of the *Iliad* corresponds to a historical reality revealed by archaeologists in the course of the last century. He concluded that heroic literature is to some extent based on history. In *The Growth of Literature* he and Mrs. Chadwick have added to the evidence for the historical occurence of genuine Heroic Ages. Where there is heroic literature, it may therefore reasonably be inferred that a Heroic Age preceded it, and that the general traits of that Age, perhaps even some of its persons, are presented to us in that literature.

The traditions of the Irish Heroic Age centre on a period in which the *Ulaid* or 'Ulidians' were predominant in Ulster and had their capital at Emain Macha, now Navan Fort near the modern Armagh. That period must therefore certainly be anterior to the early fifth century of our era, which is the latest date to which the destruction of Emain Macha and the confinement of the Ulidians to east Co. Down by the Tara dynasty can be assigned.[49] But the type of civilization described in the tales points in fact to a much earlier century. The Ulidian warriors, for instance, are consistently pictured as fighting from chariots, an early mode of fighting which is not normally attributed to the warriors depicted in any other Irish group of tales, but

49 T. F. O'Rahilly, *Early Ir. Hist. and Mythol.* 228 sq. For a suggested later date, however, for the destruction of Emain Macha see Binchy, *Studia Hibernica* II (1962), 167.

which still survived among British Celts in the first century before Christ.[50] The tradition of the Ulidian tales may therefore be provisionally regarded as being based on a real Heroic Age which existed among the Ulidians of Emain Macha perhaps about the first century before Christ.

The Chadwicks draw particular attention to the successful raiding by barbarians of a higher civilization on the borders of which they live as a factor in producing Heroic Ages. Dr. Arnold Toynbee in his *Study of History* also treats of this factor, and in addition discusses the importance of a barbarian migration, which normally coincides with it.[51] What migration, however, or what juxtaposition of a higher and lower culture, or what similar factor was responsible for the development of the Ulidian Heroic Age can hardly be discovered in the present state of our knowledge of Irish prehistory.

The warriors of the Ulidian cycle of tales are pictured as ruled over by Conchobar mac Nessa, king of Emain, and as fighting mainly on the Meath-Ulster border. The chief hero among them is Cú Chulainn, the Achilles of Ireland, who deliberately prefers for his fate a short life and long fame to long life and little fame.[52] One or other of two

50 C. O'Rahilly, *Táin Bó Cúalnge from the Book of Leinster* (1967), ix-xii.

51 I, 92 sq.; II, 94 sq., 346, 356; V, 234 sq., 252. The volume in which Dr. Toynbee treats specifically of Heroic Ages had not been published when this booklet was in preparation.

52 J. Strachan and J. G. O'Keeffe, *The Táin Bó Cúailnge from the Yellow Book of Lecan with Variant Readings from the Lebor na hUidhre* (1912), 550-572.

similar destinies had awaited Achilles, who by deciding to fight on at Troy tacitly chose in the same way as Cú Chulainn.[53]

The central tale of the cycle is *Táin Bó Cúailnge* (The Cattle-spoil of Cooley). It tells how Cú Chulainn (The Hound of Culann), while still a youth, held up an army of Connacht invaders while awaiting the arrival of the other Ulidians, who were perforce inactive because of a strange illness which used to attack them periodically, the *ces noínden* or 'nine-days illness', traced by modern anthropologists to a primitive couvade ceremony.[54] After the first injury inflicted by Cú Chulainn on the Connacht army, their king Ailill, husband of the more famous and forceful Medb, asks the exiled Ulidian Fergus, who is guiding the invaders, 'What manner of man is this Ulster Hound of whom we have heard?' This question enables the narrator, without spoiling the unity of the whole, to work in a delightful account of Cú Chulainn's *mac-gnímrada* or 'boyhood deeds.'

Among the many concepts in the Irish Táin which seem to go back to primitive Indo-european beliefs reflected also in the Greek Iliad are the *lúan* (or *lón*) *láith* 'champion's light' (also *lón gaile*, 'light of valour'), which plays around Cú Chulainn's head in battle,[55] the rising up of

53 *Iliad* I, 416; IX, 411-415.

54 For a different interpretation of this episode see T. Ó Broin *Éigse*, X (1963), 286-99; see also the same author on the word *cess*, *op. cit.*, XII (1967), 109-14.

55 Strachan-O'Keeffe, *op. cit.*, 59, 1956; cf. *Aided Con Culainn* 'The Death of Cú Chulainn' (RC, III, 177, 131); etc. In the *Iliad*

rivers to protect Cooley against the Connacht army,[56] and the occasional appearance of gods to help or oppose warriors in battle.[57]

Two main versions of *Táin Bó Cúailgne* have come down to us, a mainly Old Irish version, based on ninth-century oral tellings of the tale, and a Middle Irish version, known as the Book of Leinster version,[58] which seems to be an almost purely literary composition based on the manuscript form of the mainly Old Irish version. This Middle Irish version was probably first written about the year 1100, and is preserved in the Book of Leinster, which was compiled about the year 1160. It also appears with various modernisations in several later manuscripts, and though in

---

V, 4-7, XVIII, 206-227, similar divine lights shine from the heads of Diomedes and Achilles. The Roman centurion, who, according to L. Annaeus Florus (c. A.D. 130), struck terror into the Moesi by carrying a flaming brazier on his helmet, was doubtless aware of this barbarian belief (I. Zwicker, *Fontes Religionis Celticae*, 71-72).

56 Strachan-O'Keeffe, *op. cit.*, 205, 886, 905, 910, 1035. Cf. the rising of the Scamander against Achilles to save the Trojans, *Iliad* XXI, 234 sq. According to modern Munster folk-tradition certain rivers used to grow small to enable men of noble blood to cross them: see D. Ó Cróinín, *Dánta Árd-teistiméireachta* 1949-50 (1949), p. 56 (note on line 89 of *Caoineadh Airt Uí Laoghaire*). In Irish hagiography the river Brosnach rises against the King of Tara and his army at St. Cíarán's request (C. Plummer, *Vitae Sanctorum Hiberniae* I, 225, Vita Sancti Ciarani de Saigir, §xviii).

57 Strachan-O'Keeffe, *op. cit.*, 1713-1757, 1805. *Iliad* passim.

58 Ed. C. O'Rahilly, *op. cit.*, with English translation.

style it is less natural and direct than the mainly Old Irish version, its unity, fullness, and freedom from contradiction make it the version to-day preferred by poets and retellers of the story.

The mainly Old Irish version,[59] according to Thurneysen's masterly analysis of it in his *Irische Helden- unp Königsage*, 96 sq., seems to consist of two Old Irish texts first written down in the early ninth century and, in the eleventh century, clumsily joined together by a compiler. This compiler added certain episodes told in the Middle Irish of his day, of which the most famous is *Comrac Fir Diad* (The Fight with Fer Diad), which tells how Cú Chulainn slew in single combat his friend Fer Diad, who was one of the Connacht champions. The compilation is preserved, incomplete, in *Lebor na hUidre* (The Book of the Dun Cow), which was written at Clonmacnois about the year 1100, and also, with different lacunae, in the fourteenth century Yellow Book of Lecan. The Old Irish portions of the compilation are pleasingly straightforward in style, but the whole work particularly towards the end, seems to be a collection of notes rather than an attempt to record the story as really told.[60] It is marred by the inclusion of doublets of certain episodes,[61] and even by contradictions,

59 Ed. Strachan-O'Keeffe, *op. cit.*

60 For criticism of this opinion see Foreword p. 7.

61 In her analysis of the growth and structure of TBC C. O'Rahilly (*op. cit*, xix, n. 3) draws attention to a similar feature— 'The prominence of repeated formulas, passages and themes'—in the Homeric poems, as noted by G. S. Kirk, *The Songs of Homer*, pp. 72-80.

such as the death of Findabair, daughter of Ailill and Medb, at line 2928, and her marriage to Cú Chulainn, at line 3682, as the result of the peace made by Ailill and Medb with the Ulidians.

Fled Bricrenn (Bricriu's Feast) and *Scéla Mucce Maic Dá Thó* (The Story of Mac Dá Thó's Pig) are the other two stories which definitely mark the Ulidian cycle as a Heroic cycle in the sense in which the Chadwicks understand that word. Both tell of combats at feasts, following wordy argument between rival warriors, such as Posidonius Apamensis (c. 135– c.50 B.C.) assures us used really to occur among the continental Celts of his day.[62]

In one of the tale-lists mentioned on p. 19, the title of the first of these stories is given as *Feis Tige Bricrenn* (The Feast of Bricriu's House). In the oldest manuscript version, that in *Lebor na hUidre*, transcribed about A.D. 1100, it is entitled *Fled Bricrend ocus in Curathmír Emna Macha, ocus in Bríatharchath ban Ulad, ocus Tochim Ulad do Chrúachnaib Aí ocus Cennach ind Rúanada i nEmain Macha* (Bricriu's Feast and the Emain Macha Champion's Portion, and the Word-Combat of the Ulsterwomen, and the Ulstermen's Journey to Crúachain Aí, and the Warrior's Bargain in Emain Macha). This long title indicates the main episodes of the story: (1) the feast prepared by Bricriu, a well-known trouble-maker; (2) the rivalry between Loíguire Búadach, Conall Cernach, and Cú Chulainn as to who will be awarded the portion reserved for the best champion;[63]

62 Zwicker, *l.c.* 17.

63 In the *Iliad* (VII, 321) Agamemnon at the evening meal honours Aias for his combat with Hector by giving him 'long

40

(3) the corresponding word-combat between their wives for precedence; (4) the journey to Crúachain Aí in Connacht to have the warriors' claims judged by Ailill and Medb, their testing there in combat with magic cats and the indication given by Medb that she has judged Cú Chulainn the best warrior of the three, followed by their subsequent testing in Cú Roí's palace in west Munster by other magic beings and the definite awarding by Cú Roí of the champion's portion to Cú Chulainn; (5) Cú Roí's subsequent visit to Emain Macha to make the justice of his award evident to all by means of *Cennach ind Rúanada* (The Warrior's Bargain).

None of the extant manuscripts, as Thurneysen has pointed out (*Heldensage*, 447 sq.), preserves for us a complete text, but by use of them all a version of the story as told in the eighth or early ninth century may be restored.[64]

Classical scholars are familiar with the description of Priam's house in Book VI of the *Iliad* (ll. 242-250):

> This magnificent house was fronted with marble colonnades, and in the main building behind there were fifty apartments of polished stone, adjoining

back-pieces' carved from a five-year-old bull which had been sacrificed. This may be compared with 'the rich piece of roast sirloin that had been given Menelaus as the portion of honour' in *Odyssey* IV (Rieu's translation, 1945, p. 64).

[64] An edition based on all the manuscript texts was published by Henderson in 1899 as Vol. II of the Irish Text Society's series. For comment and indication of the interpolated portions, see Thurneysen, *l.c.*

each other, where Priam's sons slept with their wives. His daughters had separate quarters, on the other side of the courtyard, where twelve adjoining bedrooms had been built for them, of polished stone, and well roofed in. Priam's sons-in-law slept with their loving wives in these. [65]

The description of the house built by Bricriu, with which *Fled Bricrenn* opens, shows the same interest in the palaces of heroes. Instead of Greek construction in marble and polished stone, we naturally, however, find the native Irish use of wood, while in literary style the sobriety and restraint of the Greek is replaced by Celtic imaginative exuberance:

Bricriu of the Bitter Tongue had a great feast ready for Conchobar mac Nessa and all the Ulidians. He was a whole year preparing for the feast. He had made an elaborate house for the serving of the feast. That house had been constructed by Bricriu in Dún Rudraige on the model of the Branch-red palace at Emain Macha; but it excelled all houses of its day in material and artifice, in beauty and architecture, in pillars and frontals, in splendour and richness, in grace and nobility, in railings and door frames.

Now this house had been made according to the plan of the Tech Midchúarta. [66] It had nine cubicles from fire to wall: each bronze frontal was thirty feet

65 E. V. Rieu's translation (1950), 123-124.
66 The banqueting hall at Tara.

in height and was overlaid with gold; and a royal cubicle had been constructed for Conchobar in the front of that palace higher than all its other cubicles. Conchobar's cubicle was decorated with carbuncles and every other sort of precious gem. It shone with gold and silver and carbuncle and colours from many lands, so that in it night was as bright as day. The twelve compartments of the twelve Ulidian chariot-warriors had been constructed around Conchobar's. Moreover the artifice displayed was equalled by the quality of the material which had been brought to make the house. A wagon-team had been employed to bring each post, and seven of Ulster's men of might to fix every board, and thirty of Ireland's leading craftsmen to make the house and arrange it.

A sun-room belonging to Bricriu himself had been made on a level with Conchobar's and the champions' cubicles. And that sun-room had been fashioned with specially marvellous ornaments and artifices, and glass windows had been placed looking out of it on every side; and one of those windows had been fashioned above Bricriu's own cubicle so that from his cubicle he could look out with a clear view over the great house; for he knew that the Ulidians would not permit him to enter the house.

By threats of the use he would make of his bitter tongue if his invitation were refused, Bricriu persuaded the Ulidians and their wives to come to his feast; and though he himself did not enter the house, by speaking separately to his

43

principal guests before each of them entered it, he succeeded in awakening their desire for precedence and for the champions' portion, as he had planned. The episodes which follow, leading up to *Cennach ind Rúanada* have already been briefly referred to on pp. 40-1.

Cennach in Rúanada itself tells how Cú Roí came in the form of a giant to guarantee that Cú Chulainn would be admitted by all to be the greatest Ulidian warrior, in accordance with the judgment already given in the preceding episode of *Fled Bricrenn*. The *cennach* or 'bargain' was that if a warrior were permitted to behead Cú Roí on the night in question, Cú Roí would be permitted to behead that warrior on the night immediately following. On successive nights a Ulidian warrior accepts the challenge. Cú Roí on each occasion picks up his severed head and walks away. Muinremor, Loíguire Búadach, and Conall Cernach fail to keep the compact, by not appearing on the second night. Cú Chulainn, when his turn comes, gloomily lays his head on the block; the giant strikes him gently with the blunt side of the axe and says: 'Rise up, Cú Chulainn. None of the warriors of Ulster or Ireland can now claim (?) to be equal to thee in valour, or bravery, or truth. The sovranty of the heroes of Ireland is thine from this hour forth, and the Champion's Portion undisputed; and thy wife shall always enter the banqueting-hall before the women of Ulster.'

Cennach ind Rúanada is the oldest known version of the beheading motif, which is of interest to Arthurian scholars by reason of its appearance in several Arthurian tales. The finest of these is the fourteenth century alliterative English

44

poem known as *Sir Gawayne and the Green Knight*, in which the beheading motif forms the central theme.

The other Ulidian story which tells of wordy argument at a feast corresponds even more closely than *Fled Bricrenn* to the Celtic trait referred to by Posidonius; for in it, as in Posidonius's statement, the warriors actually come to blows as the result of their rivalry. The story is entitled *Scéla Mucce Maic Dá Thó*. It exists in an Old Irish version dating from c. A.D. 800 and, a fourteenth or fifteenth-century modernisation of it. Only the Old Irish version has been published in full.[67] It is a fine specimen of the old abrupt style of story-telling, with some speech-poems interspersed. *Scéla Mucce Maic Dá Thó* is one of the few hero-tales which does not mention Cú Chulainn; in it Conall Cernach takes Cú Chulainn's place as the chief champion of the Ulidians.

The quarrel under consideration took place at a feast prepared by Mac Dá Thó, king of the Leinstermen, for the Ulidians and the men of Connacht. Ailill and Medb, on the one hand, and Conchobar mac Nessa, on the other, had asked Mac Dá Thó for a famous hound which he owned. Fearing to offend either party he had promised the hound to both, and by inviting both parties for the same day he hoped that the problem would be solved by the rival parties themselves, without compromising intervention on his own part. The main portion of the feast consisted of a huge pig: 'Sixty milch-cows have been

67 The best edition is that by R. Thurneysen (Dublin, 1935). Mrs. N. K. Chadwick adds an English translation to her edition in her *Early Irish Reader* (1927), pp. 16-24.

kept feeding it for seven years;[68] but it was out of rancour it used to be fed, in order that the men of Ireland might be slaughtered by reason of it.'

The question was asked how the pig should be divided. Bricriu was present and suggested that it should be divided 'in accordance with battle-victories' (*ar chomramaib*).

'Let it be so,' said Ailill.

'Good,' said Conchobar: 'we have lads in the house who have travelled over the border.'

'You will have need of your lads to-night, Conchobar,' said Senláech Arad from Crúachain Con Alad in the west: 'often did I cause their buttocks to be wet with the bog-water of Lúachair Dedad; often was one of them left with me like a fat beef.'

'The beef you left with us was fatter,' said Muinremor son of Gerrgenn, 'namely your own brother Crúaichniu son of Rúadlom from Crúachain Con Alad.'

These opening taunts set the tone for similar boasting by other warriors among the guests, whose tauntful thrusts and parries must have delighted early audiences. The taunts of *Scéla Mucce Maic Dá Thó* are worded more roughly and vigorously than the long leisurely taunts which mark the meeting of famous warriors in the *Iliad*.[69] Cet's and Conall's respectful greetings to one another in paragraph 15 of the tale are likewise far more primitive in tone than

68 With the exaggeration contrast the restraint apparent in Greek descriptions of feasts, such as those referred to *supra* n.63.

69 The meeting of Achilles and Aeneas, for instance, *Iliad* XX, 177 sq.

corresponding courtly exchanges in the *Iliad*.[70]   This meeting of Cet and Conall forms the highlight of the story. It offers a fine example of the sudden magnificent external response to a difficult situtation which is a feature of all heroic traditions.

Cet, the chief Connacht champion, had by his taunts successively shamed several Ulidian claimants to the honour of dividing the pig. He had just settled himself to carve it when Conall entered the hall.

The Ulidians joyfully welcomed Conall, and Conchobar removed his hood from his head and waved it.

'I am glad that our food has been prepared', said Conall. 'Who is apportioning it?' 'That has been granted to the man who is doing it,' said Conchobar, 'namely Cet son of Mágu.' 'Is it true, Cet,' said Conall, 'that thou art apportioning the pig?'

Then Cet said:

Conall is welcome,

Heart of stone,

Fierce heat of a lynx,

Brilliance of ice,

Red strength of wrath,

Beneath bosom of a warrior

Who is wound-dealing and battle-victorious.

Thou, the son of Findchóem, art comparable to me!

And Conall said:

Cet is welcome,

Cet son of Mágu,

70 Hector's speech to Aias, for instance, followed by interchange of gifts, after their long duel (*Iliad* VII, 287 sq.).

> Place where dwells a champion,
> Heart of ice,
> Tail of a swan,
> Strong chariot-warrior in battle,
> Warlike ocean,
> Lovely eager bull,
> Cet son of Mágu!

'Our meeting with one another will make all that clear,' said Conall; 'our parting with one another will make it clear; it will be talked of by drovers and will be attested by cobblers (?); for roped (?) heroes will march to fierce battle; the two chariot-warriors will wreak slaughter in return for slaughter; man will step over man in this house to-night.'[71]

'But move off from the pig,' said Conall. 'And what would bring thee to it?' said Cet. 'Truly,' said Conall, 'to seek admission of battle-victory for myself: I shall give thee one instance of battle-victory, Cet,' said Conall: 'I swear by that by which my people swear, since I took spear in hand I have never been without slaying a Connachtman every day and plundering by fire every night, and I have never

71 This 'rhetoric', following the lines in archaic alliterative metre, is, like all such rhetorics, hard to understand, and perhaps not in every detail translated (see n. 48 supra). The manner of Cet's address and of Conall's reply is probably based on ancient heroic tradition; for a Tartar chieftain in the last century could show his respect for a distinguished visitor by the utterance of obscure extempore verse (see H. M. and N. K. Chadwick, *The Growth of Literature*, III, 187).

slept without a Connachtman's head beneath my knee.' 'It is true,' said Cet: 'thou art a better warrior than I. But if it were Ánluan who were here, he would match thee with battle-victory for battle-victory. It is bad for us that he is not in the house.' 'But he is', said Conall, drawing Ánluan's head from his belt; and he hurled it on to Cet's chest so that blood flowed over his lips.

Then Cet left the pig and Conall sat down by it.

Conall's hurling at Cet of his brother Ánluan's head is perhaps more barbaric than anything described in the Iliad, though Achilles' action in Book XXII, when he dragged Hector's naked corpse behind his chariot, gloating over his victory before the eyes of Hector's aged parents, is essentially as horrifying to civilized minds.

As is so often the case with Irish manuscript versions of an oral tale, the recorder of *Scéla Mucce Maic Dá Thó*, having presented one fine passage more or less as it would have been told to an audience,[72] ends his version with a condensed summary of the succeeding events,[73] which include a battle between the disappointed Connachtmen and the triumphant Ulidians in the house and outer court, the obtaining of the dog by the Ulidians and their use of it to help in the pursuit of the Connachtmen, and the death of the dog, impaled on the shaft of Ailill and Medb's chariot.

That the living tradition of the story was an oral one is suggested not alone by differences between details in the

72 For criticism of this opinion see Foreword p. 7.

73 For a plausible explanation by G. Mac Eoin for such an ending see Foreword p. 8.

version preserved for us to-day and similar details referred to in two old poems appended by Thurneysen to his edition of the ninth-century tale but also by the apparent inclusion of the tale, under the title *Argain Meic Dá Thó* (Mac Dá Thó's Slaughter), in the two main lists of tales which *filid* should be able 'to tell to kings and noblemen.'[74]

In a review of Thurneysen's *Irische Helden- und Königsage*, Wolfgang Schultz (ZCP, XIV, 299) claimed that the Irish Heroic tales are essentially Mythological and objected to their being treated as distinct from the Mythological tales. More than twenty years later T. F. O'Rahilly in his epoch-making *Early Irish History and Mythology* likewise insisted on the mythological nature of the Heroic tales:

> Actually (he writes, p. 271) the Ulidian tales are wholly mythical in origin, and they have not the faintest connexion with anything that could be called history apart from the fact that traditions of warfare between the Ulaid and the Connachta have been adventitiously introduced into a few of them, and especially into the longest and best-known tale, 'Táin Bó Cualnge.' Cúchulainn, who in the Táin is assigned the role of defender of the Ulaid against their invaders, can be shown to be in origin Lug or Lugaid, a deity whom we may conveniently call the Hero, provided we bear in mind that he was a wholly supernatual personage, and not a mere mortal. The other leading characters, such as Cú Roí, Fergus, Bricriu and Medb, are likewise euhermerized divinities.

74 See *supra* pp. 18-19.

Only in nature do we normally find divisions between classes which impose themselves absolutely. In the works of man, on the other hand, classes commonly overlap and distinction between them is largely a matter of convenience. It may well be that Cú Chulainn and Bricriu were originally divine figures, while Cú Roí still, even in the stories, retains much of his divine nature, and Fergus and Medb, though clearly regarded as human by the story-tellers, can to-day be readily recognised by mythologists as deities whose original divinity had been forgotten.[75] Mythologists therefore, may well prefer, with Schultz and O'Rahilly, to insist on the mythological aspect of the Heroic cycle. The student of literature, on the other hand, will prefer, with Thurneysen and the Chadwicks, to insist on the realistic human treatment of its characters and the general historicity of the background against which they are depicted.

In many of the tales connected with the cycle the historical element may be of very slight importance indeed. These tales are classified with the Heroic cycle merely for reasons of convenience, and may equally well be assigned to other cycles. *Seirglige Con Culainn ocus Óenét Emire*, is a case in point. It has already been mentioned among the Mythological tales on p. 32. *Tochmarc Emire* (The Wooing

75 The word 'euhemerisation' is better reserved for conscious presentation as human beings of characters whom tradition still commonly regard as divine. The euhemerising of Núadu and his companions by Irish men of learning, referred to *supra*, p. 20, may thus be distinguished from the forgetting, even in story-lore, of the original divinity of Fergus and Medb.

of Emer) is another example. It is known to us to-day from
a partially lost tenth-century recension, which contains
Old Irish strata, and a twelfth-century recension based on
it. *Tochmarc Emire* tells how Cú Chulainn, whose three
faults were that 'he was too young, too brave, and too
beautiful,'[76] was tested first by Emer herself in a riddle-
contest,[77] and secondly by Emer's father Forgoll Manach
(doubtless originally chief god of the Fir Manach tribe, the
Irish equivalent of the Gaulish Menapii), by means of an
overseas expedition, which in origin was probably an
expedition to the otherworld. A female warrior called
Scáthach, living beyond the Alps, trains Cú Chulainn in
warrior feats in the course of this expedition in which
marvellous incidents abound. The atmosphere of marvel
which gives its tone to this part of the story enabled it to
live on in the post-Norman period when romantic tales
were in fashion in Ireland, and the thirteenth-century
Foglaim Con Culainn (Cú Chulainn's Training) is a modernisation of the Scáthach portion of it. *Foglaim Con Culainn*

76 Cf. van Hamel's edition, §6 (in his *Compert C. C. and Other
Stories*, 1933, p. 22).

77 The use of riddles to test brides and suitors, as in Cú Chul-
lain's wooing of Emer, in Finn's wooing of Ailbe, and in a closely
connected Donegal folktale, is not confined to Ireland. The
Tartars have this theme in many stories (H.M. and N.K. Chadwick, *The Growth of Literature* III, 153, 158); and in Russia in the
last century testing the suitor by riddles was in some districts a
living custom (*ib.* II, 211-214). The Wooing of Ailbe and the
Donegal folktale will be referred to in the booklet in this series to
be entitled The Ossianic Lore and Romantic Tales of Medieval
Ireland.

is one of the few Cú Chulainn tales which were still popular with peasant audiences in the eighteenth and nineteenth centuries. In this it resembles the closely connected tale of how Cú Chulainn, without knowing it, or only half knowing it, slew Conlaí (later Conláech), the son he had begotten during his stay with Scáthach[78]. Schultz[79] and O'Rahilly[80] believed this to be a native Irish development of an old motif inherited from Indo-european times. In Teutonic lore a similar story is told of Hildebrand and Hadubrand; and Meyer[81] and Thurneysen[82] thought that the theme came to Ireland from a Teutonic source and that it is ultimately traceable to the Persian story of Sohrab and Rustum.[83] That Schultz and O'Rahilly are right is rendered probable by the many survivals in Irish folklore of themes traceable in other Indo-european traditions whose existence in Ireland can hardly be explained by borrowing.[84]

A number of stories, most of them more or less unheroic in tone, yet loosely connected with the Heroic cycle in the

78 The oldest version, belonging perhaps to the ninth or tenth century, is entitled *Aided Áenfir Aífe* (The Death of Aífe's Only Son). That most recently recorded is perhaps the fragment written down from oral tradition about the year 1930 and printed in *Béaloideas*, IX, 57.

79 ZCP, XIV, 302.

80 *Early Ir. Hist. and Mythol.*, 62.

81 *Fianaigecht*, 22.

82 *Heldensage*, 403.

83 This view has been supported by Tom Pete Cross in *Journal of Celtic Studies* I (1950), 176-82.

84 *Duanaire Finn*, III, xliv, 156, 193-194, 446.

manner of the tales mentioned in the preceding paragraph, used to be grouped by the medieval Irish under the heading *Remscéla* or 'Foretales' to Táin Bó Cúailnge, because they describe episodes which lead up to or explain something about the Táin. Thus *Faillsigud Tána Bó Cúailgne* (The revealing of Táin Bó Cúailnge) explains how the Táin became known to *filid* in the seventh century. It is extant in three short twelfth-century versions, and in a long thirteenth-century version entitled *Tromdám Gúaire* (Gúaire's Burdensome Company). All four versions agree in stating that the Táin was an ancient tale the manuscript of which had been given in exchange for the *Culmen* or 'Summit (of learning)'. This *Culmen*, to which there are several references in early Irish documents, has been brilliantly identified by T. Ó Máille[85] with the famous *Etymologiae* written in the early seventh century by Isidore of Seville. As a result of the exchange, only fragments of the Táin, it is said, could be told in Ireland in the seventh century. Ultimately the poet Senchán Torpéist (†657) learnt the whole Táin from the narration of the hero Fergus, who had taken part in it, Fergus having been miraculously restored to life for this purpose.

It has been suggested that this legend is based on a tradition that a version of the Táin was first written down in the seventh century, and Thurneysen in 1932[86] withdrew the objections which he had advanced in his *Heldensage* (p. 111) to so early a date for the recording of Irish lore in writing.

85 *Ériu*, IX, 71. See addendum by O'Rahilly, *Ériu*, X, 109.

86 *Kuhns Zeitschrift für vergl. Sprachforschung*, LIX, 9; ZCP, XIX, 209.

Some of the *Remscéla* such as the charming eighth-century *Aislinge Óenguso* (The Dream of Oengus)[87] are wholly mythological in character, and have very little connection indeed with the Táin. Another of them, the story of Deirdre, the Helen of Ireland, combines in its oldest version a realistic warrior background with a love-theme which may be mythological in origin. It explains why Fergus was in exile with Ailill and Medb in Connacht at the time of Táin Bó Cúailnge, and it is one of the finest tales of the Ulidian cycle. The ninth-century version of it, entitled *Longes Mac nUislenn* (The Exile of the Sons of Uisliu), is the earliest version extant of the theme of the elopement of the king (Conchobar's) destined bride (Deirdre) with one of his warriors (Noísiu son of Uisliu), and the consequent life of the lovers in exile. This theme became a part of the common literary tradition of Europe from its use in the story of Tristan and Isolda, which is traceable ultimately to a Celtic source.[88] Fergus, relying on a promise of Conchobar, had pledged his word to the three sons of Uisliu that they would not be harmed if they returned to Ulster from their wanderings with Deirdre in Scotland. On their return, however, Conchobar slew them treacherously, and Fergus, having burnt Conchobar's residence at Emain, retired to Ailill and Medb's court at Crúachain in Connacht.

Another of the *Remscéla*, the ninth-century *Táin Bó*

87 Ed. F. Shaw, *Aislinge Óenguso*, (Dublin 1934); Modernised by L. Mac Mathúna, *Feasta* (Samhain 1970).

88 An equally early Irish parallel to certain motifs in the Tristan and Isolda story is mentioned infra, n. 107.

Froích (Fróech's Cattle-raid), is a story which is hard to classify. Professor James Carney of the Dublin Institute for Advanced Studies in a public lecture delivered in 1953 in University College, Dublin,[89] has suggested that it is of monastic origin, and is based on a water-monster motif found in saints' lives, and on stories of the countries beyond the Alps brought to Ireland by pilgrims.[90] The first part of *Táin Bó Froích* treats of Fróech's wooing of Ailill's daughter Findabair, and is famous for its description of the beauty of Fróech as he swam in the pool in which he later fought and defeated the water-monster:

> 'Do not come out,' said Ailill, 'till thou bring me a branch from the rowan tree yonder on the bank of the river. Its berries please me.' Fróech went then and broke off a branch from the tree, and brought it back over the water. Findabair used afterwards to say of any beautiful thing she saw, that she thought it more beautiful to see Fróech coming across a dark pool, the white body, the lovely hair, the shapely face, the grey eye, the gentle youth without fault or blemish, his face narrow below and broad above, his body straight and perfect, the branch with the red berries between his throat and his fair face. Findabair used to say that she had never seen anything half or a third as beautiful as he.[91]

89 Further developed and printed in Carney's *Studies in Irish Literature and History* (1955).

90 For criticism of Carney's thesis see ed. W. Meid, *Táin Bó Fraích* (1967), vii-xvi.

91 Translation by M. E. Byrne and Professor M. Dillon, *Études Celtiques*, II (1937) p. 7, §17.

The Chadwicks in their *Growth of Literature* (I, 165) regard the Heroic Age of Ireland as having continued from the pre-historic Ulidian period to the end of the seventh century, the story of *Cath Almaine* (The Battle of Allen), fought in the year 718, and known to us to-day from a ninth-century version,[92] being treated by them as the latest in origin of heroic tales. The Ulidian tales, however, are on the whole the only Irish tales which tend to be truly heroic in spirit. The King cycle, to which *Cath Almaine* belongs, clearly represents a different category of storytelling.

The originators of the Ulidian tradition were interested mainly in heroic character, in loyalty, fidelity to the plighted word, fearlessness in the face of odds and ready external response to a difficult situation. Their best stories treat of some single episode which, while it illustrates heroic character, is often of little historic importance for the community just as the Greek Iliad tells of the wrath of Achilles rather than the history of the war against Troy or the life of the leader of the Myrmidons and the origins of his rule. King tales, on the other hand, show an interest, not primarily in heroic character, but in matters of importance for the community, the origin of peoples or of dynasties, anecdotes about famous representatives of a dynasty, accounts of battles which determined the course of history, or of incidents which explain some custom,[93] though much of

92 Modernised by T. Ó Floinn, *op. cit.*

93 Cf. 'That is why it is wrong for any man of the Eóganacht to slay a man of the Crecraige,' at the end of an eighth-century anecdote about the birth of Fíacho Muillethan, ZCP, VIII, 309.22.

the heroic outlook, heroic grandeur, heroic savagery, and heroic readiness of response to a difficult situation is to be found in certain passages of them. They represent primitive history rather than primitive literature, and seldom, therefore give the modern reader that aesthetic delight which he obtains from the best tales of the Mythological and the true Heroic cycles.

The Heroic Age remembered in Ulidian tradition is what the Chadwicks describe as the princely type of Heroic Age, such as we find in the Greek Iliad, the Sanscrit Mahābhārata, or the Teutonic Siegfried tales. This type of Heroic Age never lasts for long. The King tales of Ireland are situated in a background more akin to the non-princely type of Heroic Age which the Chadwicks have found existing for long periods in many places, and which it might be better to describe as a turblent semi-barbarous civilization with heroic tendencies.

The accounts of tribal and dynastic origins inserted in the historical tract known to-day as 'The Laud Genealogies and Tribal Histories' (ZCP, VIII, 291-388) are among the earliest specimens of the King cycle which we possess. Their archaic language suggests that they date from the eighth century. Many of them are mere references or short anecdotes, such as the anecdote which tells how Níall proved to his father Eochu that he was superior to his elder brothers in the prudence which should characterise a king. It was this Níall who established the power of the dynasty which ruled uninterruptedly in Tara from the beginning of the fifth century to the deposition of Máel Shechlainn by Brian Bórama in the year 1002.

Eochu Mugmedón was king of Ireland. Áed asked him which of his sons would be king. 'I do not know,' said he, 'till a smithy be burnt over their heads.' Thereupon a smithy was burnt. Brion, the eldest of the sons, seized the chariot and all its harness. Fíachra seized the wine-vat. Ailill seized all the weapons. Fergus Cáechán seized the pile of dry wood. Níall seized all the smith's implements, including the bellows, the hammers, and the anvil with its block. 'Truly,' said Eochu, 'Níall shall be their king, and his brothers shall serve him.' (ZCP, VIII, 304.31-38).

Others of these early origin legends remind the reader of the usual imperfect manuscript recordings by a man of learning of tales,[94] which often probably, in their living oral forms, whiled away the evening for audiences gathered round the fire of a royal residence on winter nights in the seventh century. Most famous among these is the account (ZCP, VIII, 309-312) of the birth and early life of Cormac mac Airt, semi-mythical ancestor of the dynasty of which Níall was undoubtedly a real representative.

Cormac's father Art is represented in this account as reigning at Tara. He had a Munster ally, Eógan Mór. This Eógan Mór, son of Ailill Mosaulam (king of Munster) was foster-brother, or uterine brother, of Mac Con, a long involved account of whose life precedes the account of the birth and early life of Cormac here under consideration. In the account of Mac Con's life it had been told that he won the kingship of Tara and all Ireland by slaying Art,

94 See Foreword p. 7.

king of Tara, and Eógan Mór at the battle of Mag Mucruime in Connacht.

The night before that battle Art went with a hundred and fifty warriors to the house of Olc Aiche, whose daughter Achtán 'was the most beautiful woman in Ireland.' Achtán's father Olc Aiche used to drink, out of a huge vessel, the milk provided by a hundred cows. Two of Art's men failed to carry the vessel to give a drink to Art; but the girl was able to carry it unaided. She distributed the contents to Art and his men, and was advised that fortune would be propitious if she were to give herself to the king, but she refused to do so without her father's consent.

> Olc Aiche comes. 'Where is my drink?' he said. She fills the vessel with milk for him. 'I recognize my little vat,' he said, 'but it is not my milk, the first milk. Where is my drink?' said he: 'this is not it.' The girl tells him. 'What did Art say to thee?' he asked. 'He has said to me: "Fortune would be propitious provided thou wert to go with the king."' 'It would be better for thee to go,' said he. 'I too should like that,' said the girl, 'provided thou didst approve.' 'Good will come of it,' said Olc Aiche, 'provided that thou bear whatever progeny he leaves; and the progeny which thou mayest bear shall be kings of Ireland for ever. Let a feast be prepared for the king by thee, to wit, fifty oxen, fifty boars, five-thousand loaves, and fifty vats full of wine.'[95] All this was brought to Art the next

95 A difficult sentence has here been left untranslated.

day; and the girl went with them, accompanied by fifty girls; and that food was distributed by Art; and the girl sleeps with him that day, and a tent was made around them, and she repeats her father Olc Aiche's words to him, and she demands a sign for herself, and Art gave her his sword and his gold thumb ring and his assembly array, and they bid goodbye to one another with great sorrow; and the girl was pregnant with Cormac grandson of Conn.

Shortly after his birth Cormac was carried off from Achtán by a she-wolf, who suckled him with her cubs. A famous trapper called Luigne Fer Trí found him and fed him for a year. Achtán having discovered this, went to Luigne Fer Trí and explained to him who the child really was. He advised her to hide the child, lest Mac Con should kill it. She therefore took Cormac to the north of Ireland to his father Art's foster-father Fiachna. Fiachna enclosed Cormac in a vessel made of yew covered with a purple cloak, lest he be killed by the hands of the people welcoming him.

When Cormac was thirty years old, assisted by his grandfather's magic, he went to Tara on an auspicious day. There he found a woman weeping.

'Why is the woman weeping?' asked Cormac. 'She is weeping,' said the steward, 'by reason of a judgement passed by the king to her disadvantage, to wit, that her sheep are forfeit for stripping the herbs of the queen's garden.' 'It would be more fitting,' said Cormac, 'that a shearing should be given for a stripping: the man who passed that judgement never passed false judgement before,' said Cormac, 'let me go to him.'

Mac Con realised that the false judgement he had passed indicated that the period destined to him for kingship had come to an end and that Cormac should succeed him. 'He raised his knee up' as a sign of homage, and Cormac began to exercise kingly functions in Tara in his place.

The theme of the rearing of the rightful heir in a distant place, far from his enemy, followed by his recognition and the winning of his inheritance, is widely spread in place and time. It is known to schoolboys in many countries through the legend of Romulus, the founder of Rome, which agrees with the Cormac story in the incident of suckling by a wolf. Herodotus in the fifth century before Christ told it of Cyrus, founder of the Persian empire, in a form which students of Greek mythology recognise as being closely related to the legend of Perseus, the legend of Neleus and Pelias, and the story of the birth of Cypselus, tyrant of Corinth (B.C. 655-625). In Irish tradition it occurs in many forms, the story of the youth of Finn mac Cumaill being the best-known example.

Several later versions of the Mac Con and Cormac incidents referred to above are described or mentioned by Dr. Myles Dillon in his *Cycles of the Kings*, 16-25. The *fili*-tale, *Cath Maige Mucruime* (Battle of Mag Mucruime), mentioned in both the long tale-lists referred to supra p. 19, would doubtless, as told orally in the ninth and succeeding centuries, have narrated some or all of these incidents less summarily and without the incoherences which mar them in the extant versions.[96]

Stories about Cormac often impress the reader as being

96 See Foreword p. 7.

stories in the true sense of the word, told to delight rather than to instruct. In one of them, the twelfth-century *Echtra Chormaic i dTír Tairngire*, 'Cormac's Journey to the Land of Promise'[97] (exant also in an Early Modern version entitled *Faghdil Chraoibhe Cormaic mhic Airt*, 'The Finding of Cormac son of Art's Branch'), he visits the otherworld, a journey to which by his uncle Conlae, on the invitation of a fairy lover, is recorded in the eighth-century *Echtrae Chonlai Choím maic Cuind Chétchathaig* (The Journey of Conlae the Fair son of Cond of the Hundred Battles).[98] Conlae, unlike Cormac, never returned. In another, the tenth-century *Esnada Tige Buichet* or 'Sounds of Buichet's House'[99](extant also in an eleventh-century verse recension), there is a charming account of how Cormac, having seen his future wife Eithne engaged in the menial tasks of milking cows, drawing water, and cutting rushes, fell in love with her. O'Rahilly in an interesting article on Buchet the Herdsman (*Ériu*, XVI, 7-20) discusses the mythological origin of *Esnada Tige Buichet*, and Dr. Myles Dillon in his *Early Irish Literature* (p.83) compares the Irish story to the 'Indian legend of Sakuntalā made famous by Kalidāsa.' [100]

97 Modernised by T. Ó Floinn, *op. cit.*

98 Modernised by T. Ó Floinn, *op. cit.*; the most recent English translation is by J. Carney, *The Capuchin Annual* (1969), 162-64.

99 Ed. D. Greene, *Fingal Rónáin and other Stories* (1955); modernised by T. Ó Floinn, *op. cit.*; the most recent English translation is by Carney, *op. cit*, 165-67.

100 In a recent analysis of this tale J. Carney (*op. cit.*, 169) would 'class it with certain other tales as part of the Irish political "scripture"'.

As other specimens of origin tales in the King cycle we may mention: the origin of the Leinster dynasty, entitled *Orguin Denna Ríg* (The Destruction of Dinn Ríg), extant in an imperfectly narrated ninth-century version;[101] the origin tale of the Ulster sept known as Dál mBúain, which, in its eleventh-century form,[102] tells of the tragic love of Baile Binnbérlach mac Búain (Baile of the Musical Speech son of Búan) for Aillenn of Leinster; stories concerning Conall Corc, reputed founder of Cashel, the chief stronghold of Munster, of which the eighth or ninth-century *Longes Chonaill Chuirc* (Exile of Conall Corc) is an example; the origin tale of the Munster Eóganacht families narrated summarily in eighth-century Irish in the Laud tract already mentioned,[103] and incorporated in another form in *Cath Maige Léna* (The Battle of Mag Léna), a well-told Early Modern King tale, composed probably by a Munster poet for some O'Sullivan chieftain in the thirteenth century; the long early-twelfth-century semi-historical compilation which tells of the origin of the Bórama tribute claimed from the Leinstermen by the kings of Tara, and of various efforts to exact it. The Bórama compilation includes the tragic tale of Fithir and Dáirine which, from the story point of view, is better told as an episode in the late-twelfth-century *Acallam na Senórach* or 'Colloquy of the Ancient Men' which will be described in the booklet in this series

101 Ed. D. Greene, *op. cit.*

102 Edited by E. O'Curry, *Manuscript Materials* (1878), 472 sq. Modernised by T. Ó Floinn, *op. cit.*, a summary of the tale is given by Dillon, *The Cycles of the Kings*, 27-9.

103 *Supra*, p. 58. Cf. Meyer's edition, ZCP, VIII, 312-313.

to be devoted to the Ossianic Lore and Romantic Tales of Medieval Ireland. One of the poet's tale-lists includes *Tochmarc Fithirne ocus Dáirine, dá Ingen Túathail* (The Wooing of Fithirne and Dáirine, the two Daughters of Túathal) as a separate tale. In the form in which we have it, as an episode in longer compilations, it tells how the king of Leinster won for his wife the elder daughter of Túathal, king of Tara.[104] The king of Leinster did not love her. Having therefore confined her to a dwelling in the forest, he wooed the younger daughter. The sisters met, and one died of shame and the other of grief for her. Warfare resulted, till finally, according to the Bórama tract, the Leinstermen agreed to pay a large *éraic* or fine, which was the origin of the tribute known as the Bórama.

Exigencies of space forbid mention of many other tales of the King cycle. One group of them, however, occupies so important a place that it deserves brief treatment here. The group in question consists of traditions about seventh-century or early-eighth-century events. A fine early example is the tragic *Fingal Rónáin* or 'Slaying by Rónán of One of his own kin', extant in an imperfectly preserved but clearly once well-told tenth-century version.[105] *Fingal Rónáin* narrates the tragic slaying by Rónán king of Leinster (†624) of his beloved son Máel Fothartaig, who had been falsely accused by his stepmother of trying to ravish

104 The versions do not agree as to which was the elder, Dáirine or Fithir.

105 Ed. D. Green, *op. cit;* modernised by T. Ó Floinn, *op. cit.* and summarised (with partial translation) by Dillon, *op. cit.* 42 ff.

5

her.[106] Anecdotes and tales connected with the east-Ulster king Mongán mac Fíachnai (†625), or with the Connacht Gúaire (†662), famous for his generosity, afford other examples of this class of tale. Still another example is the story of the Hebridean Cano son of Gartnán (†688), one aspect of which has been already discussed on pp. 14-5.[107] Several tales connected with the battle of Mag Rath, fought in 637, afford further examples of the group of stories under consideration: the most famous of them is the twelfth-century *Buile Suibne* or 'Madness of Suibne', which tells how Suibne, an east-Ulster king, through the curse of a saint went mad from terror in the battle and lived in the wilderness among birds and wild animals; it contains some of the finest nature poetry in Irish literature. The latest in origin of these seventh and early-eighth-century stories are those concerning Cathal mac Finguine (†742) and his contemporaries or close predecessors: they include *Mór Muman ocus Aided Cúanach maic Cailchéni,*' Mór of Munster and the Death of Cúanu son of Cailchéne' (extant in a ninth-century version); the amusing *Aislinge Meic Con*

106 Máel Fothartaig is therefore the Irish equivalent of the Greek Hippolytus, against whom his stepmother Phaedra made a similar accusation.

107 The story of Cano is of special interest to scholars for the close parallel it contains to certain motifs in the Tristan and Isolda story. This parallel has been discussed by Dr. Myles Dillon, *op. cit.,* 79–80, and more recently by R. Bromwich, Trans. *Hon. Soc. Cymmrodorion* (1953), 53, *Studia Celtica* I (1966), 154–55, and by J. Carney, *Studies in Irish Lit. and History,* 215–17. Cf. also *supa* n.88.

Glinne or 'Vision seen by Mac Con Glinne' (extant in two twelfth-century versions), in which Cathal is pictured as afflicted by a demon of gluttony; and the tale of the Battle of Allen already referred to on p. 57.

Though tales either definitely belonging to the King cycle, such as *Serc Gormlaithe do Níall Glúndub* (Níall Glúndub's Love for Gormlaith, the former slain by the Norse in 917),[108] or at least closely related to that cycle, came into existence sporadically in later times when circumstances resembling those of the ancient King period favoured their growth,[109] it may be said with truth that the originating of King tales came to an end in the course of the first half of the eighth century. This cessation of legend-origination about kings may be partly connected with the more orderly behaviour of the kings themselves; for even to-day stories tend to be narrated of those who are rebels

108 We know the plot of this story, the title of which is given in both of the two main tale-lists, from various references in annals. Moving poems connected with it, clearly from an Early Modern version of the story, are the only traces of a text of it which survive to-day.

109 The dramatic rise to power, at the end of the tenth and beginning of the eleventh century, of Brian Bórama, ancestor of the O'Briens, and his victories over the Norse, gave rise to literary compositions and folktales which have been admirably discussed by Dr. A. J. Goedheer in his *Irish and Norse Traditions about the Battle of Clontarf*, Haarlem, 1938 (The folktales are mentioned on p. 71). Some traditions from the Norse period of Irish history, and some later traditions, such as those of the rise to power of the O'Donnells, Maguires, and MacSweeneys, have been briefly discussed by G. Murphy, *Glimpses of Gaelic Ireland* (1948), 35-43.

against reason rather than of those who follow the ways of law. It is doubtless, however, to a still greater extent due to the growth of a more critically rational outlook on the part of the recorders of kingly tradition, whose function it was to preserve memory of the past for succeeding generations: annal-making and the tendency to rely on written documents had brought legend-origination to an end among the recorders of kingly tradition.

Of all the King tales *Togail Bruidne Dá Derga* (The Destruction of Dá Derga's Hostel) is the finest. The best-known version of it is that narrated mainly in ninth-century Irish and preserved to-day in the early-twelfth-century *Lebor na hUidre* and other manuscripts. This version, as Thurneysen has shown (*Heldensage*, 623 sq.), is apparently due to an eleventh-century redactor who compiled it, not over-skilfully, from two ninth-century texts known to him. It tells of the slaying of Conaire the Great (son of Etarscél), king of Tara at some ancient period before the rise to power of the dynasty to which the Níall already mentioned on p. 58 belonged. Conaire is represented as a model king, who was induced by the hidden influence of the *des síde* to violate his *gesa* (religious prohibitions, or taboos), thus bringing upon himself an inevitable doom. This tale is Greek rather than Irish in its mounting sense of impending tragedy, as its hearers, and ultimately Conaire himself, realise that the *gesa* are being violated one by one, some unconsciously, others consciously but against Conaire's will. And, greatest tragedy of all, those who play one of the most important parts in slaying Conaire are his own foster-brothers, bound to betray him by reason of a general oath sworn to a British pirate, with no thought of the particular application in which it might result.

Togail Bruidne Dá Derga is linked to the Ulidian cycle both by its heroic spirit and by the presence in it of some of the warriors who normally appear only in that cycle. Conall Cernach, for instance, normally appears only in Ulidian tales, but he is depicted as having been with Conaire when Dá Derga's hostel, in which Conaire had taken refuge, was destroyed. This is the account, typical of the heroic spirit, of how his father Amairgin received Conall when he arrived home from the battlefield on which his lord had been slain:

> Conall Cernach escaped from the hostel; and one-hundred-and-fifty spears had pierced the arm on which he had his shield. He travelled till he reached his father's house, with half his shield on his arm, and his sword and the fragments of his two spears in his hand. He found his father before the enclosure surrounding his stronghold in Teltown.
>
> 'Swift are the wolves that have hunted thee, lad,' said his father.
>
> 'Our wounds have come from a conflict with fighting men, old warrior,' said Conall Cernach.
>
> 'Thou hast news of Dá Derga's hostel,' said Amairgin. 'Is thy lord alive?'
>
> 'He is not alive,' said Conall.
>
> 'I swear by the gods by whom the great tribes of the Ulidians swear, it is cowardly for the man who has escaped alive, having left his lord with his foes in death,' said Conall Cernach's father.

'My wounds are not white, old warrior,' said Conall. He showed him his shield arm. One-hundred-and-fifty wounds had been inflicted on it; but the shield which protected it had saved it. As for the right arm, it had been twice as badly used: for though the sinews of that arm held to the body without being parted, it had been hacked, cut, wounded, and riddled, since there was no shield guarding it.

'That arm fought this night, lad,' said Amairgin.

''Tis true, old warrior,' said Conall Cernach: 'many are they to whom it gave drinks of death this night in front of the hostel.'

Togail Bruidne Dá Derga is a tale which it is hard to classify. Conaire would seem to have belonged to the people known as Érainn, who in historical times were confined to Co. Cork in south Munster, but had once been widely spread over Ireland; there is reason to believe that the Ulidians themselves were closely related to them. T. F. O'Rahilly has shown[110] that, according to various sources, Laginians (in historical times the men of Leinster), as well as British pirates, were responsible for Conaire's death. He holds with probability that the tale of his death in a burning hostel, and of the apparent burning of the homesteads of Meath by the *des síde* which led to it, may (apart from mythological elements) ultimately be traced to vague memories of the first night of the Laginian invasion of Ireland from Britian, in the third century before Christ, told from the point of view of the Érainn who ruled in

110 *Early Irish History and Mythology*, 119-120.

Tara at the period.[111] O'Rahilly also[112] gives good reason for believing that the story of the Destruction of Dinn Ríg, already mentioned on p. 64, represents a tradition of the Laginian invasion told from the Laginian point of view. 'We are fortunate,' he writes (*l.c.* 140), 'in possessing a double account of this invasion, one of them told from the viewpoint of the invaded, the other from that of the invader, so that we are enabled the more easily to realize the tragedy on the one side, the triumph on the other.'

LATER DEVELOPMENT

In the course of the twelfth century Irish literature was enriched by several versions of classical stories, such as *Togail Troí* (The Destruction of Troy), an Irish adaptation of the *De Excidio Troiae* attributed to Dares Phrygius, and *Imthechta Áeníasa* (The Wanderings of Aeneas), based on Virgil's Aeneid. The Latin texts were freely altered, however, to suit Irish taste. Some of Virgil's most beautiful passages, the metaphor, for instance (*Aeneid*, XII, 473-478), by which Iuturna is likened to a swallow flying through the halls of a rich man's house in search of food for her young, are omitted by the adaptor, while elsewhere he inserts descriptive passages modelled on Irish saga tradition. It is doubtful, however, whether these classical adaptations

111 The Ulidian tale known as *Togail Bruidne Dá Choca* 'The Destruction of Dá Choca's Hostel' (extant to-day only in a thirteenth or fourteenth-century version, and discussed by O'Rahilly *l.c.* 130-140) clearly represents a different tradition of what is essentially the same story.

112 *l.c.* 103-117.

ever entered into the living tradition of storytelling in Ireland.

Storytelling in the Heroic and Kingly traditions seems, with some exceptions, to have lost its vitality in the changed Ireland which resulted from the Anglo-Norman invasion of 1175, partly, it is probable, because that invasion put an end to the kingly *óenaige* already mentioned on p. 18, where the *fili* would have above all found hearers who would have both expected and appreciated it. To the Finn tales and Romantic tales, which became the principal tales in the petty lordships which characterised medieval Ireland, after kingly Ireland had ceased to exist, it is hoped to devote a special booklet in this series under the title The Ossianic Lore and Romantic Tales of Medieval Ireland.

INDEX OF TALE-TITLES

Binchy, D. A.: 'The Background of Early Irish Literature' *Studia Hibernica* 1, Dublin 1961.

Dillon, Myles (ed.) : *Early Irish Society*, Dublin 1954. *Irish Sagas*, Dublin 1959. (transl.) *Gods and Heroes of the Celts* by Marie-Louise Sjoestedt, 1949.

Jackson, Kenneth H.: *The Oldest Irish Tradition: A Window on the Iron Age,* Cambridge 1964.

Mac Cana, Proinsias: 'The Influence of the Vikings on Celtic Literature' *Proceedings of the International Congress of Celtic Studies held in Dublin 1959,* Dublin 1962; *Celtic Mythology,* London 1970.

O'Connor, Frank: *The Backward Look: A Survey of Irish Literature,* London 1967.

The following booklets have been published in this series: